SEX *and* SENSIBILITY

SEX and SENSIBILITY

TEN WOMEN EXAMINE THE LUNACY OF MODERN LOVE... IN 200 CARTOONS

Cartoons and Essays by

Roz Chast

Barbara Smaller

Liza Donnelly

Julia Suits

Carolita Johnson

Ann Telnaes

Marisa Acocella Marchetto

Kim Warp

Victoria Roberts

Signe Wilkinson

Edited by Liza Donnelly

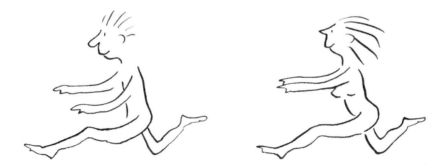

TWELVE

New York   Boston

Twelve
Hachette Book Group USA
237 Park Avenue
New York, NY 10017

Visit our Web site at www.HachetteBookGroupUSA.com.

Twelve is an imprint of Grand Central Publishing.
The Twelve name and logo are trademarks of Hachette Book Group USA, Inc.

Printed in the United States of America

First Edition: April 2008
10 9 8 7 6 5 4 3 2 1

Library of Congress Control Number: 2007937152
ISBN-13: 978-0-446-19815-8
ISBN-10: 0-446-19815-3

For Michael

"We love because it's the only true adventure."

Nikki Giovanni

Contents

Introduction

SO MUCH IS HAPPENING AT BREAKNECK SPEED, it's difficult to know how to behave. When Jane Austen wrote *Sense and Sensibility,* she may have felt similarly. She wrote of the conflict between *sense*—the concern for decorum and worldly things; and *sensibility*—the attention to inner life and the senses. Her concerns were woman's place in her world, and the notion that while fitting in may be important, the inner world of emotion and creative thought can be elevating. While her world was not changing at the crazy speed of today's, it must have been confusing.

Even now we attempt to adapt, fit in, make money, make love, make laughter. This book speaks to similar issues—fitting in and listening to inner thoughts—and brings them to contemporary discussion. Here, collected in cartoons and essays, are creative thoughts of ten women who, in many ways, chose *not* to fit in, *not* to go the way of sense. Instead, they chose to tap into their sensibilities, with humor. Austen made use of humor in her writing, for laughter often loosens strictures as it opens eyes. It helps us deal with the wackiness of life and love.

As it gets progressively more difficult to keep up with what's going on, escaping becomes a pleasant idea. Turning off the BlackBerry is a pleasant idea. But then, think of what you'll miss. And there might not be support groups for e-mail addiction in Tibet. Better to keep the BlackBerry on, and enjoy the ride. It's a technological theme park, and the absolute best ride is the Love Roller Coaster. Screaming and laughing may be the best (and only) solution. Take a cartoonist with you for the ride; I promise you it will be even more fun.

Cartoonists are journalists, but don't "report" in the traditional way. We use humor to shed light on craziness, on cultural trends, politics, human behavior. Many Americans now get their news from Jon Stewart and Stephen Colbert. No wonder: So much of the news is grim, they give us permission to laugh. And while many just leave it at that, the effectiveness of humor—when it is good—can bring reality into clarity more succinctly. While naysayers bemoan the fact that Americans' news comes from the likes of Stewart and Colbert (and Tina Fey, until she left *Saturday Night Live*), this is good news for humorists. In 1941, E. B. White wrote in his introduction to *A Subtreasury of American Humor,*

The world likes humor, but it treats it patronizingly. It decorates its serious artists with laurel, and its wags with Brussel sprouts. It feels that if a thing is funny it can be presumed to be something less than great, because if it were truly great it would be wholly serious.

The treatment of wags, or humorists, has remained the same for decades. *The New Yorker* magazine brought some respectability to wags, beginning as a humor magazine in 1925 with the likes of E. B. White, Katherine Angell, Dorothy Parker, Helen Hokinson, James Thurber, and S. J. Perelman, to name a few. Humorists were understood to be artists and thinkers who made us laugh. Dorothy Parker's work, while hilarious, verged on tragedy much of the time. Her artistry points to the clear thin line between comedy and tragedy. When we laugh at our plight, its reality often cuts into the soul more quickly.

And what is closer to our soul than love? Cartoonists draw about war, famine, and corruption. But when they draw about love, we really listen. Love is the universal language, and the universal headache. The War Between Men and Women has gone on so long, it's tempting not to call it a war anymore. Aren't wars supposed to have a beginning, a middle, and an end? The term *Perpetual State of Misunderstanding Between Men and Women* may be a better—although less poetic—way of describing the situation. And do battling factions in a war make love along the way? Temporary Truces or Meetings-at-Large-Round-Tables-in-Geneva don't really equate with "making love." Nor do weekends at Camp David (although we never really know what happens at these gatherings, do we?). What goes on between men and women is complicated, and cannot be simply described as a "war" or "battle." Cartoonists know this, and it is their job to ferret out the details to make us laugh and see what is really going on. We pick at the details to find the truth.

For most of the history of the world, the chronicling of love has been done—or at least recorded—by men. (Perhaps that is why it has been called a "battle." Men love battles.) Shakespeare, Byron, Keats, Twain, Hemingway, Updike, Thurber all wrote of love and sometimes made us laugh. Thurber brought *The War Between Men and Women* back into parlance with his series of cartoons under that title. But it *was* a war between the sexes in 1950s America. Men and women were being forced into roles they did not want to fill. We "attacked" each other, each gender thinking the other was forcing the issue. When the roles were challenged—when we realized that women should not have to be perfect, sweet homemakers and weigh 110 pounds and that men should not have to be strong and silent and earn tons of money—the "battle" changed to something else. It is no longer a war, but continuous communication—a Sexual United Nations, with representatives from all walks: lesbians, gays, transsexuals, feminists, traditionalists, and maybe even eunuchs. When all sides of the battle are given the floor and heard, as women began to be heard in the 1960s (and had to a certain extent in the 1920s, but it was short-lived), then the war becomes a conversation.

The discourse can get heated sometimes, and it can come to fisticuffs. But the dialogue is there. What happens when the dialogue changes format? When we talk via the Internet, instead of face-to-face? What happens when we make love via cell phone? Do the rules change? Are we going to see a breakdown of communication? A resurgence of war, a technological skirmish, a BlackBerry Battle? Not if women *and* men have a voice. Not to say misunderstanding will disappear, but it won't be a "battle." The new rules of the twenty-first century make it more confusing, but they increase our dialogue. And now the discussion firmly includes women's voices (unlike Jane Austen's time—she wrote anonymously). And while it may be much more interesting to cover a war than to cover a peace, it is the subtlety of the situation that calls for chronicling from cartoonists. Cartoonists of both sexes.

· · ·

When I was little, my mother loved to recite the following Dorothy Parker verse:

<u>News Item</u>

Men seldom make passes

At girls who wear glasses.

Nearsighted since the age of nine, I had to wear glasses if I wanted to see the world clearly. My mother, also visually impaired, loved to tell me that she walked around half blind for most of her young-lady life because, she said, she wanted the attention of men. It's the same with shoes: High heels may make a woman's legs look more beautiful, but they put a girl in a very precarious, vulnerable position. Seeing clearly, walking strongly, were not feminine. Why would we need that when men can "see" for us and "support" us? For so many years, they have been the movers and seers.

I also found that being quiet was a desired feminine trait. It's a gamble to show smarts when you are a woman—men don't want you to be smarter. If you were a little bit attractive, it didn't matter. You got attention for your looks. So I stayed quiet for a very long time. Not surprisingly, in fact, until I got married. My lessons in early life were that women didn't need to see, think, speak, or walk. Being a child of the 1960s, I wasn't content with this situation. I found I could apply my intellect privately and somewhat anonymously as a cartoonist. People laughed at what I created. What power. My drawings were lightly satirical, so I did not risk stepping over the ladylike boundary. Thus I subconsciously chose cartooning as a career—a field of work where I could be opinionated and funny, and not get chastised. I could be powerful and still get a man!

That boundary, the social code of feminine behavior of which all women are aware, has been crumbling. Women have been chipping away at it for decades. The bits of crumble became visible in the post-Victorian era. Women began speaking their minds, not only about the right to vote, but about the right to wear pants, the right to go out into the world, the right to not be so "good." Many fought the battle privately with their spouses; others did so publicly in the effort to gain suffrage. Some—and they are less well known—worked quietly at drawing boards and writing tablets, creating humor to expose injustices. Florence Seabury, Francis Whitcher, Marietta Holley were once well-known humorists, but now forgotten. They attacked the status quo by ridiculing their own gender, seeking to open women's eyes to their position and behavior. Women cartoonists, such as Lou Rogers and Edwina Dumm, drew political cartoons for the vote, seeking to bring new voices into the all-male-dominated art form. Women wanted change, and humor was one way to chip away at social restrictions and conventions. It was a bumpy road—not only was the publishing industry male-dominated and reluctant to publish women writers and cartoonists, but society's acceptance of what was funny did not include any female tradition. What women found funny was not always the same as what society found funny, and vice versa. The style in which they wrote differed, as did the topics they wrote about. But their humor made some women see more clearly. They wore pants and sensible shoes (some of them), and they provided glasses for nineteenth-century women.

In this atmosphere, Dorothy Parker emerged. An avid writer in childhood, she stumbled on a job at *Vogue,* the very female tower of fashion and acceptable behavior. Parker wrote captions to photographs, and inserted subversive, irreverent humor. Remarkably, this went unnoticed (perhaps because it was so unexpected), but she was soon fired. Her wit soon found a home at *The New Yorker* in 1925, riding the urban flapper wave. Allowed to smoke, drink, party, and crack jokes, the flapper was a "buddy" to her man. This was Parker. As a woman at the original Algonquin Round Table, her sharp tongue was noticed and celebrated, as was her writing. Her volumes of verse were best sellers, and she became one of the most famous women of her time. Parker's stories, much like the nineteenth-century female humorists', took sharp jabs at women, and laid bare what society was doing to women. Parker's work has never gone out of print. A testament to its timelessness, the longevity of her writing reveals the notion that things have not completely changed between the sexes.

Battle of the sexes is a phrase of unknown origin. James Thurber made the concept famous, and his prose often centered on the tension between men and women—Thurber's Walter Mitty character symbolized the downtrodden male, belittled by a domineering woman. This is how 1950s America was treating strong, opinionated women, and humor took hold of it to great success. The flapper was gone, a victim of the Depression and World War II, and women were to return to the home, be domestic, and stop thinking for themselves. This was fuel for humor. Much humor of this period—including cartoons—used the stereotypes of domineering women and bimbo secretaries. In contrast with the playful, congenial times between the sexes in the 1920s, relations became strained, and most gains by women humorists were buried. Collections of humor rarely—if ever—contained women writers. Cartoon collections printed work by the handful of women, but generally used cartoons of theirs that upheld stereotypes. While there were around eight women cartoonists at *The New Yorker* in its early years, in the 1950s there were two, and in the 1960s, none. The cartoonist Barbara Shermund, whose cartoons in *The New Yorker* echoed Parker's sensibility, faded away into obscurity. Parker went to Hollywood, as did so many writers, to write scripts. In the 1960s, humorists Erma Bombeck and Jean Kerr slowly began a female tradition again writing domestic humor essays. Humor narrowed into male domination, and "the battle" was described by men. Women were not considered funny—except in rare instances such as Kerr and Bombeck—and anyway, their humor was considered to be only for other women. Mae West continued to struggle with censorship. Lucille Ball broke the barrier of television, bringing her remarkable physical comedy into acceptability, but her gains as a comedian quickly slid into stereotypical "goofy wife" predictability.

This was the reality. The critique of our love lives was only described by writers of the male persuasion, whether it be in comedy, television, verse, or cartoons. The second wave of feminism arrived in the 1960s, and provided another set of (stronger) glasses. Betty Friedan, in her book *The Feminine Mystique,* describes "the problem with no name," exposing what was bothering women trapped in domesticity. Women discovered, as Virginia Woolf wrote, "a room of one's own"—a metaphorical space to think for themselves. But the constraints that prevent women from truly defining themselves as they want, and speaking as they want, linger. Creating humor requires a Herculean ability to stand outside of society, outside of those forces. It requires a freedom of intellect and an ability to stand removed from what is expected.

Humor has traditionally been an aggressive art form. While women have fit into that mold or found another way to create humor, both efforts historically met with resistance. Women weren't funny, "couldn't take a joke"—it was unladylike to be aggressive. Women lacked the intellectual freedom to create humor with their own, truest voices. Until now. What began with Francis Whitcher, and continued with Dorothy Parker, Mae West, Erma Bombeck, Lily Tomlin, Phyllis Diller, Elaine May, Whoopi Goldberg, Gilda Radner, Sandra Bernhard, Veronica Geng, Roseanne Barr, Molly Ivins, Ellen DeGeneres, Tina Fey (I could go on), today continues in so many ways in numerous female humorists. Sarah Silverman, Margaret Cho, Kate Clinton, Amy Poehler, Patricia Marx, and Maureen Dowd are creating socially challenging material. This progressive chipping away at establishment humor has brought us, more than a century later, to a time when many women now create humor in a freer way. Now we have the glasses, can break glass ceilings and crumble walls—all while making everyone laugh.

• • •

There have always been women artists. They have not always been recognized, but they were there. One of the differences with the art of cartooning—and humor in general—is that it requires an audience. One can draw cartoons for one's own amusement, but by definition the form is created for others' amusement. While women can—and have for generations—painted and sculpted in the privacy of their studios, women cartoonists have had a tough road. The cartoonist has to be aware of what others find funny, and work with that while staying true to the cartoonist's voice. And, to be published, the cartoonist has to be aware of the editor's sense of humor. Historically, newspaper and magazine editors have been men, who upheld tradition in most cases.

There was a mini explosion of comic strips by and for women in the early 1900s, brought on by the urbanization of America. This was not true in political cartoons, partly because women were considered the moral gatekeepers of society, and politics was not considered a woman's place. A handful of woman cartoonists drew for the suffrage movement, but once the vote was won, they either stopped cartooning or continued in strip work and illustration. *The New Yorker* was not afraid to publish women cartoonists. Helen Hokinson, Barbara Shermund, and Alice Harvey were a strong presence in the first ten years of the magazine (1925–1935). Each had a slightly different voice and made fun of life as a woman in the Jazz Age. Harold Ross and his wife, Jane Grant (an early activist feminist), founded the magazine seeking to reflect the new urban life for men and women. While the "funnies" made fun of working-class life, *The New Yorker* made fun of the elite sophisticates. But this group was part of a wave of change that was overcoming the country—change in humor from the folksy Plains tradition to snappy modern wit. Ross's vision for *The New Yorker* included a desire for new humor and a new visual look; and because of this openness, women artists could fit in. The city was adapting to women in new roles, and the magazine reflected that in its cartoons—publishing humor by cartoonists who happened to be women. Their work appealed to both men and women. The explosion of women who drew cartoons (from the 1890s to 1935) was short-lived. The domestication of America that followed the Depression and World War II silenced many women cartoonists or changed them from innovators to perpetuators of status quo humor.

The doors opened again (it was really more of a knocking down of the doors) in the 1970s. Women created humor within (and to a lesser extent, without) the umbrella of the second wave of feminism. This brought groups of women defining themselves with a single voice. Feminist humor questioned the stereotypes and set up a new genre of humor—one could now joke about everything feminine in a mixed audience (whether the audience liked it or not): menstruation, menopause, clitoral orgasms, bras, plastic surgery, vaginas, and the "g spot." Openly critiquing the status quo humor, and openly satirizing men, these women—and the whole feminist movement—were labeled "humorless," "unable to take a joke." Breaking barriers requires taking risks, and just as many of the female cartoonists of the suffrage movement were repeatedly lampooned, so were the feminist humorists of the 1970s. As time progressed, the "single voice" of feminist humor that dispelled so many stereotypes evolved into many individual voices. The defining category of aggressive feminist humor had done what it had to. Women now could define humor for themselves as people. No longer a group, per se, humor from women began to be humor from writers and artists *who happened to be women.*

In the cartoon world, this era brought us Nicole Hollander, Shary Flenniken, Trina Robbins, and M. K. Brown to name a few. At *The New Yorker,* a new sensibility opened the doors to a handful of women. The magazine that had not had a woman cartoonist for close to twenty years soon began publishing Nurit Karlin, Roz Chast, and myself. Of the women in this book, the 1980s brought Victoria Roberts; the 1990s welcomed Barbara Smaller, Marisa Acocella Marchetto, and Kim Warp; and the 2000s have brought us Carolita Johnson and Julia Suits. In editorial cartooning, both Signe Wilkinson and Ann Telnaes represent the very few women practitioners. These ten women, and myself, have individual voices, and represent a new phase of cartooning, bursting with female voices in cartoons, comics, and graphic novels. They speak out about everything—sex, love, politics, and—well, what else is there? Their voices are unrestrained by the barriers and restrictions of the past. Their humor is refined and raw, fresh and timeless.

In this new environment, one that brought us *Roseanne, Sex and the City,* and *30 Rock,* the nature of how we love can be openly described by women. It can be lampooned by women. How women see what is *really* going on between the sexes is fair game. Women can make fun of sex as they see it, can make fun of marriage and relationships as they see it. Not filtered through the male perspective. No longer are the jokes always about women not wanting sex, or men always having affairs; nor are they consistently about men not sharing their feelings and women crying all the time. The jokes are not always about women being the good girl or the slut, and the man being the randy philanderer and witless spouse. Stereotypes persist, but the whole subject of love and sex is more nuanced now, and the narrow bands of behavior that we have been confined to are (almost) gone. Freedom breeds creativity breeds communication. And, most importantly, freedom breeds laughter.

• • •

Add to this new freedom the fact that the outward nature of love and sex in our world is changing at whirlwind speed. Internet sex. Texting sex. Sex toys of all sorts. Threesomes. Tensomes. Unclear sexual preferences. YouTube. Amateur pornographic videos. Plastic surgery to change everything and anything one wants. Piercings in amazing places. Tattoos in amazing places. Presidential sex (or not). Abortion (or not). Priests doing unpriestly things (or not). Gay marriage. Gay divorce. Gay parents. Global warming (maybe that's not about sex). The warming of our society's sexual appetite. The lunacy of love has reached new heights. But the roller-coaster ride is still fun.

The ten voices represented in this book are rich and varied. Roz Chast shares her world of neurotic characters struggling to cope with one another. Kim Warp and Julia Suits push the envelope of lunacy to new heights. Ann Telnaes and Signe Wilkinson bring a sharp political edge to their observations, revealing from a woman's perspective that love and sex *can* be political. Barbara Smaller shows communication breakdown in all its glory. Marisa Marchetto and Carolita Johnson scrutinize human behavior with satirical acumen. Victoria Roberts's poetic whimsy brings humor to a philosophical level. We use our unique talents to tap into our sensibilities. We leave no holds barred: Men *and* women are poked and prodded. We hopefully shed light on it all. A light that, while not new, is now in the mainstream. While we are women, we speak in *human* voices. America may soon elect—much to its surprise—a president that happens to be a woman. It could take longer to see a woman in Jon Stewart's perch, or David Letterman's chair. This book, along with the increasing acceptance of humorists who are women, is a start.

I'm sure that Jane Austen would have been totally appalled at the work in this book, not to mention how I changed her title. But the sensibilities of these cartoonists lighten our world. They are mistresses of the fine art of examination; they are journalists, artists, and scientists, observing, dissecting, listening. And drawing hilarious conclusions.

Sex

IF CHARLES DARWIN HAD BEEN A CARTOONIST, he would have been so consumed with the hilarity of his subject that he would never have gotten around to writing *The Origin of Species.* You can't make this stuff up. Male birds in all their colorful glory puff themselves up to attract females, female insects eat males after sex. Mammals are less outrageous—until you get to *Homo sapiens.* The things we do to perpetuate the species! Is this truly adaptation; are we as a species evolving to a higher place when it comes to sex? Are cell phones a Darwinian modification?

Sex is everywhere now. Not that everyone is doing it, but the media makes us think everyone is doing it. And that everything hinges on everyone doing it. Buy a car because it's sexy. Drink this soda because this beautiful girl drinks this soda, and maybe you can have sex with her. Listen to this song, watch this video, wear this outfit, buy this product—and maybe you will have sex at some point in the near future. We are being bombarded with sex.

And yet it continues to be an intimate conversation between two people. It still serves a Darwinian purpose—we continue to have babies—but the purpose has evolved to amazingly creative proportions. Our desire to be close to one another in a fast-paced world has led to infinite variations on the act. And on what to use *in* the act.

So have things really changed? What has evolved is that women are openly in the conversation. Not only the conversation as to what to do in the bedroom (or boardroom or closet), but the conversation *about* the what and how we do in the bedroom. Darwin and most scientists in American history were men. Today Darwin could be a woman. Sexperts are women. Cartoonists are women. We observe, expose, and laugh just as brilliantly as men. Watch out. We will make fun of it all, in search of fun.

But *it* really hasn't changed much.

"I need a hug, but straight sex will do."

"Isn't it romantic?"

*"Are you the girl who ran the ad about being
into sales and marketing?"*

"Feel like a threesome?"

*"You don't have any time?
Try fitting Taoist sex into your schedule."*

"Do I believe in monogamy . . . why must we bring ideology into this?"

RECENTLY, I HEARD A JOKE ON *FAMILY GUY*: A mother is going to run for mayor, and someone asks, "Can a woman be mayor, or will she just menstruate all over the city?"

I laughed. There are a lot of things about being a woman that make people uncomfortable, and this naturally leads to humor. Most of this humor is only appreciated by women, though. For example, I once drew a (rejected) *New Yorker* cartoon that ultimately ended up with the punch line, from the man, "No time for sex? But it only takes five minutes!"

Actually, those were my own words, said to a man. But somehow those words sound reproachful in a cartoon when they come from a woman's lips, which is not at all what I'd intended. I'd meant it to come out exactly the way it would sound coming from a guy: innocent, wheedling, bargain seeking. So I put it in the mouth of a man.

The original basis for the cartoon was a boyfriend's reply to my telling him that sex with him was not going to happen while I was menstruating. He said he didn't mind having sex during my period, so I told him that while that was very open-minded of him, I was grumpy and crampy during my period, and didn't even want his open-minded little mug in my sights till it was over.

One of my (male) colleagues said to me, when I proposed this as a possible gag cartoon, "Yeah, right! Like *The New Yorker* would ever print a cartoon with the word *menstruation* in it! Good luck with that!" Actually, that was before I even began submitting to *The New Yorker*—I was thinking of sending it to one of the women's magazines. But why is something that more than half the population experiences for half their lives so ridiculously taboo?

I think it's because a lot rests on a woman's reproductive organs in our civilization, and this leads men to want to control what happens to our bodies. When I was in graduate school in Paris, I studied women from a socioanthropological point of view. Men tend to identify their social integrity with the bodily integrity of their women, I learned; it's a real form of hysteria. This is why rape is often used as a political tool, whether it's a politician stirring up territorial feelings with the threat of "the barbarians coming to ravage our women" or actual men systematically raping women in wartime to commit symbolic genocide by polluting the enemy's progeny.

Of course, women sometimes benefit from the protection afforded by this sometimes benignly hysterical impulse. But sometimes we don't. In this dubious bargain, we aren't even supposed to

continued on p. 22

"We 'don't have time for sex'? It only takes five minutes!"

mention our own bodily functions, much less exercise control over them. That's true of lactation, menstruation, and, in particular, birth control and abortion. The reason is simple: When we're talking about our bodies, we're really talking about men and their identity in our world. No one wants to be reminded of the thing that makes him or her feel the most vulnerable.

What I think is kind of funny, or maybe just ironic, is that women, although we have come very far since the Dark Ages, have not yet been able to articulate a discourse about ourselves that isn't simply a reaction to the control our society exercises over us. No matter what we do, we will always be a "woman" this or a "woman" that, a "female president" or a "female cartoonist." Never just the simple subject of the verb without that qualifier. Or, at least, not yet.

"Vive la différence!" was something I learned to appreciate in France. There are surely differences between men and women that inform all our reactions and points of view, especially about sex. But women are changing, and so are (I assume) men. We'll always be different, but I hope we'll laugh at different things twenty years from now than what we laugh at now.

This is one reason that I have never been interested in being a "woman cartoonist," even if I fall into that category one way or another. I prefer to be simply a cartoonist, like any other cartoonist. But there are things left to say before that will happen, and this is one of the places where they'll be said. Maybe someday, another woman will read my words and think, *How out of date and irrelevant to modern society!*

I'd love that!

Carolita Johnson

*"Not tonight. Why don't you upload the sex we had
last week and watch us on the big screen?"*

"I'll objectify you if you'll objectify me."

"That was one hell of a climax."

"If we're not going to have sex,
I'll go slip into something more comfortable."

"Sex is God's joke on human beings."

Bette Davis

"Yes, it was good for me—not as good as it was the last time,
but probably better than it's going to be the time after this."

"Hey, what do you think this is—a touch tank?"

Porn For Women

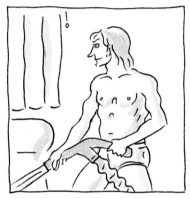

"Oh, goody! Just in time for the game!"

"*What? I thought you wanted me to get a Brazilian.*"

*"We met at just the right time in our lives,
when we both wanted something cheap and tawdry."*

"Hey, wanna get kinky and read each other's catalogues?"

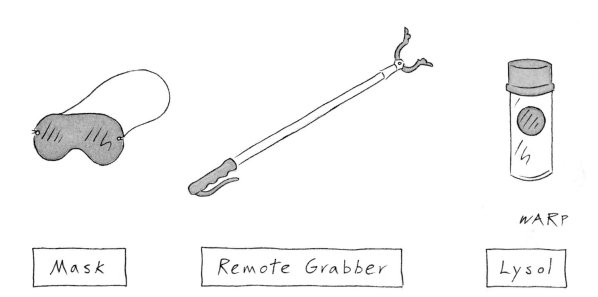

Sexual Aids For The Squeamish

Mask

Remote Grabber

WARP

Lysol

"In love? No, we're in bed."

" Tell him I've been too fucking busy—or vice versa."

Dorothy Parker

"I'd like a Chardonnay and I'm fairly certain he'd like sex."

"Do any of those fit?"

"So it's true. You really are all business."

"This patch is to stop smoking, this patch is to lose weight, this patch is to read the newspaper faster . . . and this patch turns me into your personal sex machine and the bottom patches keep my socks up."

Antisex Toys

*"Be honest, are you seeing someone else,
or did you get that from 'Men's Health'?"*

"I can't believe you booed me!"

"Oh shit, my husband wants to have sex."

"I found a porno movie in your drawer.
I guess that means you're curious about sex."

IN THE THIRD GRADE, I FINALLY SAW THE SEX EDUCATION MOVIE

I'd been hearing about for years from my older sisters. My class saw it in two separate showings, the boys in one room and the girls in another. The movie showed how the sperm grew in the man's testicles and how the egg grew in the woman's ovaries. It showed how the sperm entered the egg and a baby started to grow. It did not say or show one thing about how the sperm got from the testicles in the man to the egg in the woman. I thought maybe it jumped over?

When my mom picked me up from school, I couldn't contain my puzzlement any longer. I explained what the movie said and how it had left out the "middle" part, and asked her how *exactly* did the sperm get from the man to the woman? My sisters were in the car with me and they noticeably perked up, as I don't think the whole thing had adequately been explained to them, either. My mom, a registered nurse, visibly blanched and said, "They have a thing called sexual intercourse." Her face clearly forbade further inquiry. I decided that, to be safe, I probably shouldn't stand too close to boys until I got a clearer answer. Obviously, I was going to have to research this thing on my own.

Mom had her old nursing school text around the house, which my sisters and I furtively scoured for information. There was a small section on "marital relations" with odd questions and answers. Not at all informative, they were written in the same mysterious and obscuring language Mom had used. I don't know when I discovered the truth. But I know that by the seventh grade, when all my friends passed around a copy of *The Godfather* (page 22 in particular—the scene with Sonny and Lucy the bridesmaid), I had my answer. And not standing too close to boys still seemed like a really good idea.

Since then, I've done a lot of research, even stood next to a boy or two, and still can't believe that's really how it works. I have my own daughters now and have gone overboard with information so they won't have to turn to *The Godfather* for the truth. Thankfully, nowadays there are a bazillion books on the subject aimed at boys and girls of every age (apparently I wasn't the only one who had trouble getting a straight answer). Despite my discomfort, I promised myself that all my daughters' questions would be answered in age-appropriate language. I worried about giving them too much information, but was told that young kids don't put it all together and only retain what they can understand. However, one day, when one of my daughters was about *four,* I was driving somewhere with her and she *had* put it all together. She asked me a very astute question (that I'm forbidden to repeat) and I, being

continued on p. 50

"You want sex? Am I in an alternative universe?"

my mother's daughter after all, nearly drove off the road. But I answered. "Kinda."

I like to think of myself as not doing *those* kinds of cartoons, but the truth is I write and draw about male–female relations (or *the whole messy thing* as I like to call it) continually. In our family, we didn't talk about such things much, but my parents were always willing to laugh at any of my funny drawings, and I've always felt free to talk about anything in my cartoons. Somebody has to see if the editors are awake. And any topic that ripe with turmoil, mistakes, and misunderstandings is impossible to stay away from, even for an adult (who can't stop snickering like a seventh grader).

These days, when everyone over four knows how it all works, people still struggle to hook up and stay with the opposite sex. As grown-ups, we still turn to movies, trying to figure the whole thing out. At least in the third grade we were seeing the same thing; now, instead of seeing the same movie in separate rooms, men and women watch entirely different movies. We seem to have given up mutual understanding and make movies that appeal to one gender or the other. And I don't think we're really learning the same things about sex and relationships from old romantic comedies and porn.

For years, we've primarily seen the male point of view in cartoons. When I first saw *Cosmopolitan* as a teenager (as part of my continuing sex education), I was mystified by the cartoons. They seemed to be cartoons a man might draw, with the roles reversed (they were). They just didn't seem true to me. Sometimes you hear men say women aren't funny, but I distinctly remember *not* laughing at those cartoons. When I started drawing my own a few years later, I discovered that editors were eager for the woman's point of view, and *Cosmopolitan* became one of the first places I was published, even though we had differing ideas about how attractive the women in the drawings needed to be.

More recently, in *The New Yorker,* I did a cartoon showing a couple in bed: The woman is saying to the man, "How would you feel if I woke you up every morning wanting sex?" About a week after this cartoon was published, I received an e-mail from a somewhat miffed male reader saying that the cartoon was the female point of view and a man would see it exactly the opposite way! Yes, I know, we've been seeing the "Not tonight, I've got a headache" cartoons for fifty years. Isn't it fun to see the other side? I also received e-mails from female readers loving that cartoon and one from my parents wondering why so many of my cartoons lately were on *that* topic (as direct as ever). I pointed out that I actually did a lot of cartoons about *not* having sex, which seemed to satisfy them. And, really, since

I've inherited a bit of my mom's inhibitions and don't talk about sex much in real life, if I mention it as I sit quietly drawing in the privacy of my own home, who's going to see?

If you're a woman cartoonist, people always ask you what it's like to be a woman cartoonist. What's it like to be a woman anything? We push our breasts out of the way and try to do the job. Maybe that's why women cartoonists wear a lot of black T-shirts—hides the ink. With the same challenges as any other woman torn between motherhood and career, I feel lucky to be able to work at home and do both. Everyone brings their own life experience when they draw cartoons. If you're a woman, you have a different set of experiences to add to your pile and certainly a different perspective. Trust me, when people are always asking you what's for dinner—like you're psychic or something—it's bound to affect you.

But from all the cartoonists I've talked to—men and women—the work process is about the same. We all have scraps of paper with ideas jotted down and an intense fear of blank paper. We spend hours taking one word in and then out of a caption, researching drawings on the Internet, and trying to get the idea down to the essentials, all with the goal of a drawing that makes you laugh (out loud if possible). When my husband first saw this process, he was shocked that a finished cartoon that looks so easy can be arrived at through such apparent pain. "You make it look hard." It occurs to me that this comment could just as well be applied to relationships. We *all* make it look hard, and that's why cartoonists draw about it. It's funny no matter which side you're looking at it from. If we can see— and perhaps laugh at—what the opposite sex laughs at, maybe it will all get just a tiny bit easier.

Kim Warp

"I do have a fantasy about horse-whipping you,
but it's not a sex fantasy."

"It's after midnight, Sweetpea—no more phone sex."

"*You were right! Baseball is better than sex!*"

Sensibility

YOU HAVE YOUR IPOD, YOUR CELLPHONE, your television, your pager, your Game Boy, your digital camera, your BlackBerry. Now try to find your sensibility. It's around somewhere. With CNN on all day long, are our sensibilities enhanced or numbed?

How many more people killed today? How many more celebrities arrested? How many more movies to watch, things to buy?

While our sensibilities may be numbed to the outside world (unfortunately), our sensibilities to personal intimacies remain acute (is this Darwin again?). Everyone wants love, and we still innately know that we *have* to listen to one another in order to get and give love. Even with the TV on, we have adapted the ability to hear what our partner is really saying.

Cartoonists have highly refined sensibilities. Some say women have a keener ability in this realm, almost to the point that it has been a burden. Nineteenth-century woman was the keeper of the moral gate; her high level of sensibility was thought to best serve the home. But now this quality in women—while lampooned over the centuries—is used for everything, not just keeping us good. Running a corporation, fighting a war, directing a movie, drawing a cartoon.

We can laugh at our emotions and our reactions to one another. In all the ensuing hilarity about what you want, what I want, how you feel, how I feel, what you think, what I think, there may be room for the outside world.

But it helps to put the cell phone on manner mode.

"*I appreciate that you're trying to be your authentic self,
but why must you stomp all over my authentic self?*"

*"We both wish it was like in the movies but
I like old musicals and he likes porn."*

"I'm working on a steamy novel about a girl working on a steamy novel in a coffee shop. What are you working on?"

Victoria Roberts

"Why do we get along?"

"I'm leaving you, because you don't know why I'm leaving you."

I LIVE WITH A CARTOONIST WHO HAPPENS TO BE MALE. After twenty years in our personal cartoon gender laboratory, I have several observations about male cartoonists:

1. Male cartoonists are attention seekers. Like rock musicians, they want the eyes and ears of females.

2. Male cartoonists generally draw to amuse themselves. If they get others to laugh, that's even better.

3. Male cartoonists initially become cartoonists out of a deep-seated need to please.

4. Male cartoonists are very observant of behavior—others' behavior, not their own.

5. Male cartoonists don't really fit in, and like it that way. They don't usually wear khaki pants, or have normal hair.

6. Male cartoonists consider others—almost all others—as target practice for "witty" observations.

7. Male cartoonists don't have gender construction issues. They will do laundry and vacuum.

8. Male cartoonists will often push humor to the adolescent level.

9. Male cartoonists bring humor to almost everything, including sex (not a bad thing).

10. Male cartoonists are worriers. They worry about checks-in-the-mail and cracks-in-the-ceiling, but mostly, they worry about whether or not you are happy. And/or laughing.

While these observations can be similar to those found in female cartoonists, there are differences. The characteristics of female cartoonists are:

1. Female cartoonists are sensitive.

2. Female cartoonists use humor appropriately.

3. Female cartoonists fit in.

4. Female cartoonists never use stereotypes.

5. Female cartoonists avoid hurting others' feelings.

6. Female cartoonists are joiners.

7. Female cartoonists do have gender construction issues, and won't do laundry or vacuum.

8. Female cartoonists never stoop to adolescent humor; in fact they skipped adolescence.

9. Female cartoonists are smart.

10. Female cartoonists are always funny.

As one would expect, living with another cartoonist has its laughs. We each speak the same language, one that is at once verbal and visual, and feed off each other's individual approach to what's funny. This behavior can annoy others, particularly teenage daughters. When the joke won't stop, when it keeps getting parsed into endless variations and your daughter is about to leap out of the moving vehicle to escape her parents' self-satisfied humorfest—you know it's time to tone it down.

All cartoonists are observers and communicators: My husband and I look at people and how they behave, and use humor to expose ridiculousness in others and in ourselves. Clothing choices, word (mis)choices, food choices, social gaffes, hair issues, toe size, facial expression, dancing efforts, cooking (in)ability, fussing tendencies, you name it. This heightened sensitivity serves a marriage well, as it helps us see each other and communicate. The humor keeps the "dialogue" (if that's what you want to call it) fresh. Egos are dislodged with satire. The displacement only lasts a few seconds, but it keeps the cartoon gender laboratory—our marriage—real. However much it scares the pets and children, it's worth it.

continued on p. 67

"I'd invite you in, but my life's a mess."

I have noticed that my husband—the male cartoonist—draws for himself. While I—the female cartoonist—draw for other people. Not that he isn't aware of his audience, and not that I am unaware of what pleases me. He can spend hours at his desk just drawing away while I sit at my desk worrying about who will like what I draw. Is this social conditioning, or is it genetic? Whatever it is, it annoys me that I can't lose myself like he does. Drawing for yourself and others at the same time is a narrow line to walk. And it is particularly difficult because the audience is not visible or audible. We don't show each other our work because of the risk that it won't get a laugh. So you are forced to measure your success on how many you publish. That is not a fair determinant as to the quality of your work, because let's face it—most magazines and newspapers have one or two editors, and humor is subjective. So my husband and I "test" our humor voices out on each other through living it. *Then* we draw it.

Art and words. The two elements have to blend seamlessly, effortlessly. The viewer has to understand it all in one quick moment. Too much visual information or too many words crowds the idea and complicates the delivery. Often the cartoon tells a story, even if it is one panel. You bring your life to the story, no matter what the subject. There are characters, setting, dialogue—it's like a set. The trick, if you are living with a cartoonist, is to be able to discern what is real life and what is strange cartoon life. We both have to execute the delicate dance of words and image. And merge the absurd with the real—a daily activity for two married cartoonists.

This process of creating cartoons is the same whether you are a man or woman cartoonist. We all struggle with these issues. But what makes it perhaps a bit more challenging for cartoonists who happen to be women is that people have deeply ingrained ideas of what's funny, and how funny is presented. We are all simply *cartoonists,* not men cartoonists, not women cartoonists. But some of us have to overcome socially instilled internal and external barriers—to embrace that we are indeed funny, find a way to successfully present what we think is funny, get the notion across that what we think funny is funny, and convince others that *how* we execute what is funny works.

It is a definite advantage to have a partner who thinks you're funny. Then you both make fun of it all, together. Funny, isn't it?

Liza Donnelly

HEARALIS:
for men with empathy dysfunction.

Possible side effects: ears may fall off.

"If you love me, you'd give me your miniature umbrella."

"Blah, blah, blah."

"Blah, blah, blah."

"Blah, blah, blah."

"Blah, blah, blah."

"Are we there yet?"

Victoria Roberts

"The quickest way to a man's heart is through his chest."

Roseanne Barr

"He's really nice in an abusive sort of way."

"I wear neutered shades of beige when I'm with my wife."

"*I don't really feel like talking, but if you like I'll pick a fight.*"

"He just came through a nasty engagement."

"Now, who wanted to marry a woman he could watch sports with?"

"Say, for argument's sake, that you were called upon to do so—
could you identify my genitals from a photograph?"

"He couldn't change and I couldn't change wanting him to change."

"I don't even understand what I don't understand about men."

Maureen Dowd

"You do have a lot of feminine qualities, just none of the good ones."

"I never date—I'm too niche."

"She's a charmer, I'm a snake. We get along."

AN EXCERPT FROM

MEN ARE FROM BELGIUM, WOMEN ARE FROM NEW BRUNSWICK

When women and men say:	They actually mean:
Guy: Is this meat loaf?	**Guy:** This is meat loaf, isn't it?
Gal: Of course it is, darling.	**Gal:** Do you have a problem with that?
Guy: Mmm. It's _delicious_!	**Guy:** It's awful.
Gal: I'm so glad you're enjoying it.	**Gal:** Isn't that a darn shame.
Guy: Did you use a recipe?	**Guy:** Did you just throw all this stuff together randomly, or what?
Gal: To tell the truth, I was feeling kind of creative, so I made it up!	**Gal:** So what if I did. SO WHAT. _SO, SO, SO WHAT!!!_
Guy: Next time, don't be shy about using a recipe, O.K.?	**Guy:** It's completely inedible, that's what!
Gal: Okeydokey!	**Gal:** Your criticism stems from your own feelings of inadequacy. You should seek professional help.

"My penis is crazy busy. How about your vajayjay?"

" **A different taste in jokes is a great strain on the affections."**

George Eliot

"*Why must you know who it is, don't you trust me?*"

*"You're wasting your time, Mister Strong-and-Silent.
I'm looking for Mister Weak-and-Chatty."*

" 'I adore men, but don't always like them.' Who said that?
Or rather, who hasn't said that?"

"*I wonder which will fade first—your tan or your animal magnetism.*"

"I'm sorry, Jon, but Henry's perfect. Not only does he make me laugh, he makes me omelets and he makes me come."

"We need __something__. I'm just not sure it's tango lessons."

*"I was looking for a soul mate, now I'm just looking for someone
I don't want to strangle."*

"In my experience you don't really know someone until you divorce them."

*"He makes a big deal about holding the door open for me,
but leaves the toilet seat up."*

I DIDN'T CHOOSE TO BE A CARTOONIST. I was one, from the beginning, starting from when I was about thirteen. I don't remember a time when I didn't draw, and accompany said drawings with a title and what became eventually a caption.

What drives my work is dialogue. I think about it all the time. To me a person's vocabulary and phrasing are a fingerprint. The way people describe themselves through their choice of words and syntax—that is my passion.

I rarely make up a character. They walk into my work, and out again, of their own volition. My characters have been with me for about thirty-five years, and I might say I know them well. But I think, the way it works, is that they know me better.

Although I enjoy drawing immensely, and love watercolor and pattern, I never think about artwork too much. Drawing is a tool to bring life to the folks who inhabit my cartoons, and to give them a setting.

I am extraordinarily grateful to work with these characters, and am grateful to be working in this medium—cartoon—which I find fulfilling, efficient, and complete.

I work in a female voice, my own. It is as natural to me as being of the female gender.

Victoria Roberts

Victoria Roberts

"I had a mother who cooked and a father who ate—
now there's an ideal relationship."

"What theme will unite us tonight?"

"*I'm either just like your mother, or just like my mother, it can't be both.*"

"Always a couch potato, never a Swede."

"I like you, Charles. You're more substance than spin."

"So when are we going to talk about talking?"

"How's your relationship?"

Women

WHAT DOES IT MEAN TO BE A WOMAN? We can have babies. Does that define us? Is that it? Some think so; in fact, it has been said that this is the reason why we aren't funny. Serious business, having babies. Bearing children colors everything. Perhaps it does, but women are able to override and change the color to any shade we need. Or to make it black-and-white. And while men don't *get pregnant* (yet), they have children and raise them. The seriousness of the endeavor is for all to share.

Women have repeatedly attempted to break out of the box, and with each generation this is met with humor (and resistance). While we crash that glass ceiling, we continue to have plastic surgery on every inch of our bodies. Botox, liposuction, tummy tucks, silicone. The expectations, the complicated dance we do with society never ceases to provide fuel for laughter. It's no wonder the "What do women want?" question persists. We want freedom, we want control, but we also want the freedom to relinquish control when we want to relinquish control. That's pretty clear, right? We want to make men happy, but we want to make ourselves happy.

High heels, Birkenstocks, bra burning, push-up bras, stay-at-home moms, working moms, free sex, monogamy. Women don't speak with one voice, which is great for humorists. While each feminist wave brought great material for laughter (although it was hard to take), the open push–pull of the twenty-first century is even funnier. Whether the other half wants to hear it or not, we make fun of menstruation and menopause. What's new is that women are creating the laughter at themselves, not just accepting the laughter society chose to force.

Dorothy Parker wrote of women in such a brutally funny way, it shed light on how we behave. We can provide ourselves—and everyone else, too—with the best medicine.

Laughter is much less expensive than liposuction, and infinitely less painful.

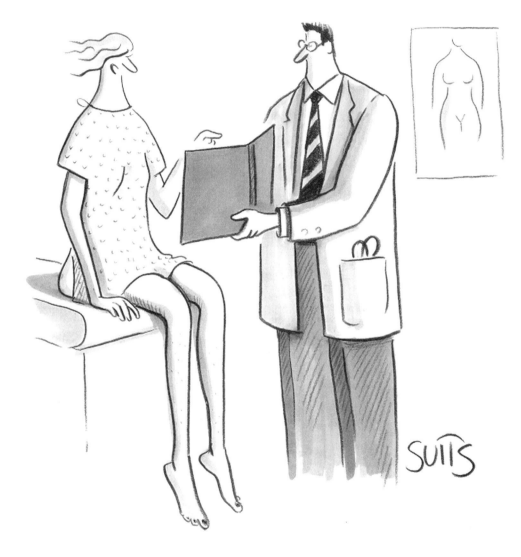

"*Yes, I think I'll have the vagina/boob makeover.*"

"*I'm taking a week off and having everything lasered.*"

"What do I have that goes with my new relationship?"

"She doesn't talk about it, but she's happily married."

WHAT'S FUNNY ABOUT BEING A WOMAN?

Well, nothing if you gauge it against all the obstacles and inequalities women are faced with every day. Fewer legal rights, forced marriages, and second-class social standing confront women from around the world. Even in so-called civilized modern societies, women earn less and have to put up with more in the workplace. Take a look at the number of females in the US Congress and you'd think the Nineteenth Amendment just passed a few years ago. Turn on the news and count the number of women commentators discussing the day's political developments; apparently there just aren't many women around who have an understanding of these things. There seems to be an endless supply of white guys in suits who do, though.

So is it any surprise that we women aren't seen as having the same sense of humor as our male counterparts? We're so busy dealing with this stuff that watching three guys bonking heads or nyuk, nyuk, nyuking just doesn't appeal to us. We have more important issues to aim our pens at. Okay, I admit that after hanging around with my male colleagues for an extended period of time I do tend to crack up more easily at toilet humor. Must be a type of cartoonist Stockholm syndrome.

Ann Telnaes

"*I want you to make me look single.*"

"Yes, I realize that we are free agents, but I have to take on the additional risk of pregnancy and am more susceptible to certain sexually transmitted diseases, so I think you should pay for the movie."

*"I want something that's assertive for the office,
but nonthreatening for an evening out."*

"Oh, c'mon . . . he's not the only CEO in the sea."

"*The lesbian world welcomed me with open arms . . . I can't just leave.*"

Victoria Roberts

"Pretty undies keep the soul intact."

"My brain could kick her brain's butt."

"In my sex fantasy, nobody ever loves me for my mind."

Nora Ephron

*"I plan on having a baby someday, but I'm waiting
for the right technology to come along."*

"Is there a feminist backlash, bitch?"

"*They say finding a man is twice as hard at fifty,*
so I'm doubling up in my forties."

"He told me he loves me and wants to marry me and spend the rest of our lives together, he's so manipulative."

"Well, I think making six figures can be very girlie."

" A woman's a woman until the day she dies, but a man's only a man as long as he can. "

Jackie "Moms" Mabley

"Been there. Done him."

Victoria Roberts

"I said, 'I'll cross that bridge when I get to it.'"

"Stay away from me, Haines, or I'll fire you <u>and</u> stab you!"

"You're an addict? That's perfect because I'm an enabler."

"He's heterosexual, but he works out as much as a homosexual."

"That's it, no more dates with men I meet in the Barnes & Noble self-improvement section."

"*Some of my best friends are married.*"

"I found a great house that actually comes with a house-husband."

WHEN I AWAKE EACH MORNING, I never think, *How can I use my art to inflict the female point of view on my readers?*

For starters, there is no single female point of view, as my friend Margaret reminds me every time she delivers her opinions—which, sadly, often diverge from my own. In addition, cartoonists generally enjoy anonymity in all ways including sex. Back when people still wrote letters, much of my hate mail would cheerfully begin, "Dear Mr. Wilkinson."

Lastly, I was brought up in a family and a religion that asserted the fundamental equality of all people—shockingly, even women. From an early age, I believed in my bones that I could be every bit as dense as any man. I have a substantial body of drawings that proves it. Consequently, I wasn't out looking for a cartoon girls' club.

Still, as my day job demands humor about war, politicians, and the dictates of men in robes who wish to run—and ruin—my life, this book offered an amusing respite. It allowed me to appear in the company of gifted women whose work makes me laugh. And, of course, believing we are equal before God doesn't mean we all react the same before a suddenly leaking toilet. There are obvious differences between the sexes, as the many volumes of cartoons on the subject attest. It is still true that most of those differences are chronicled by male cartoonists, since most of the cartoonists are still men. Even when those fine human beings make an insightful point I wish I'd thought of, satisfaction comes not from having a man portraying women (however sympathetically) in cartoons. Satisfaction comes from being the person wielding the pen.

Signe Wilkinson

"Don't be so nice to me—it keeps me in the same place."

"Bill's my type exactly—no strengths, all weaknesses."

"No, I will not first show you my vagina."

"My biological clock is on snooze."

"My first apartment, my first husband."

*"I'm not looking for something that makes a statement,
I'm looking for something that mumbles."*

Lunacy

LOVE BREEDS INSANITY. It makes us nuts. When we are in love, we can't think clearly. To find the love, we don't think clearly. We do wild and foolish things to find, get, and stay in love. This is not new. After the love-induced folly comes the lunacy of pairing up. What men do drives us crazy. What women do drives us crazy. Shakespeare knew it. Jane Austen knew it. Mark Twain and Dorothy Parker laughed at it.

And in our efforts to please one another and ourselves, we step over into wild and crazy behavior. Is this a neurotic reaction to all the fast-paced changes? Is this the response to not understanding what the hell is going on? The stress of *trying to fit in* can be unbearable, so lunacy seems appropriate. It gets attention when your e-mail goes unanswered.

Humor is lunacy contained. Cartoonists easily create lunacy: It is their nature to push the envelope. If the situation itself is lunatic, we just reflect that, with embellishments. By seeing the foolishness, humorists show us ourselves by making us laugh. If we are laughing, and once the happy tears clear, the truth can be spotted. Have a backup plan—save it on your flash drive, add it to your bookmarks, store it in your Photobucket. You have to be quick before you start crying.

"*Okay. I guess we can die now.*"

"*What . . . ever . . .*"

"I'm getting new boobs for graduation."
"Hey, me, too!"

"A lot of these so-called 'suits' are wearing women's underwear."

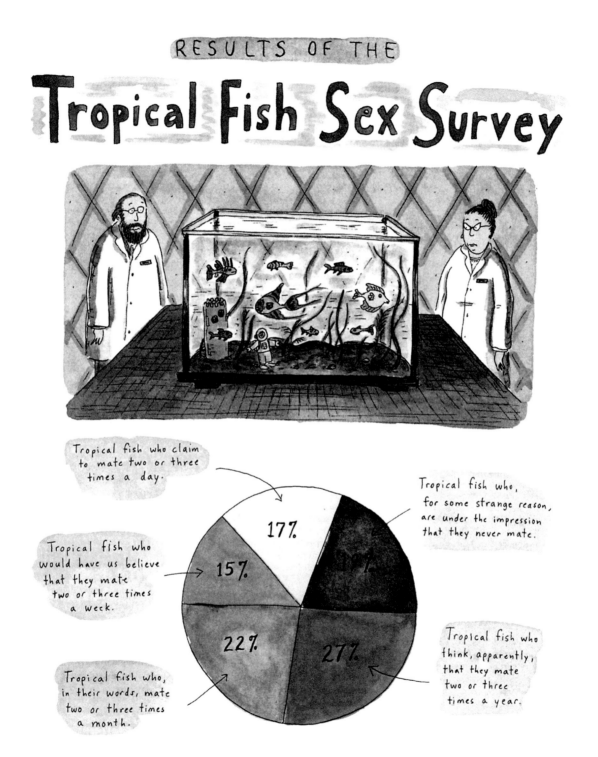

"And this song goes out there to any girl who might consider sleeping with me."

"*A clit ring! Honey, you shouldn't have.*"

"Now try forks."

Victoria Roberts

"We are all sex-obsessed today, because there isn't any decent group life left."
—W. H. Auden

I spend a lot of time staring at walls, out windows, thinking. A child of artist parents, I grew up a watcher, not so much a talker. Cartooning is a comfortable form of commentary for me. It's also a way for me—a sociable person who often feels isolated in my current life—to connect with more people. I love the process of thinking, writing, drawing, and editing—conveying a hard-to-define something in just the right way. Weigh the sounds of individual words, the combinations of words, the rhythm, the feel, the balance, the off-balance—then draw an image that works well with the caption, that's what I do.

"I just want to ridicule everything!" —Lucy talking to Charlie Brown, by Charles Schultz

I did not attempt cartooning until well into middle age (or is it early old age?). It seemed the answer to a life crisis born out of usual life dissatisfactions and frustrations, but especially the monstrous doings of the Bush White House: as a mother, US citizen, and earthling, I was/am mad as hell. I began drawing cartoons and soon realized I could poke fun at massive idiocy and personal, first-person idiocy.

   This felt good. When I was invited to come up with cartoons for this book, I thought, *Sex—great. A favorite subject of mine. I can make fun of sex.* But the challenge for the book was to be funny yet somewhat pithy. Well, pithy doesn't come to me as easily as truthy. Light, amusing, and *truthy.* I think a lot of the cartoons I did for the book will ring true for many readers.

"Sex...it has something to do with acting ridiculous in the dark." —Matt Groening

During the creative process I am not consciously female, male, or anything but a wee human, with a wee brain, making light of the human condition. Finding new little tricks with language and a pencil—that is the challenge and joy of cartooning.

"Love is like racing across the frozen tundra on a snowmobile which flips over, trapping you underneath. At night, the ice-weasels come." —Matt Groening

Julia Suits

"Goodnight sling, goodnight lair, goodnight noises everywhere."

FIRST DATE

FIRST ANNIVERSARY

"*I brought him home to meet my mother, and now she's dating him.*"

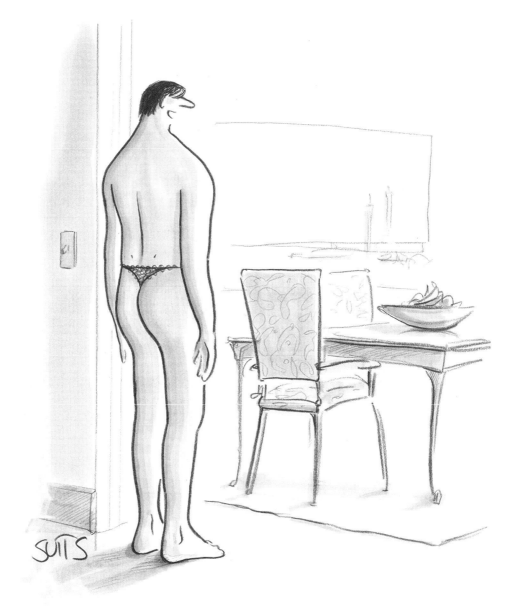

"*Honey, come see how much better I look in this than you do.*"

"Norman, if I should go first—promise me you won't try on my pantyhose after I'm gone."

"Oh, baby! Yes! Don't stop! Yes! Keep criticizing the way I drive!"

"So we're e-mailing lesbian erotica to one another, and then I find out 'she' is a Republican congressman from Ohio."

"You will do foolish things, but do them with enthusiasm."

Colette

"Discus or shotput, what's your poison?"

"I'm popping out for some anonymous sex.
Can I bring you back anyone?"

"*So <u>now</u> will you take me to the pot o' gold?*"

"You are <u>really</u> fun to be with."

"Men are completely nuts. Women can't understand their behavior because men themselves have no clue as to what they are doing."

Merrill Markoe

"You're a sexpert? I'm a sexpert, too!"

"Well, I finally got Michael to go to Paris with me."

WHAT'S FUNNY ABOUT BEING A WOMAN

Breasts are funny, because they kind of stick out in this certain way.

The way I fuss about my hair is funny. It used to be too oily. Now it's too dry. I'm always buying products for it like it's a princess's hair, even though most of the time I'm in my house. It's ridiculous! I probably fuss so much because I'm a woman and my hair is long. Although maybe if I were a guy with long hair, I'd be just as fussy and maybe if I were a woman with short hair I'd be less fussy. I don't know this.

Let's say I'm about to walk through a door, and a man insists on opening the door even though he's holding nine packages and I'm not holding anything. I tell him, "No, no, don't bother," but he insists. I say, "No, seriously! I'm fine!" Suddenly, we're in a screaming fight about whether or not he's going to hold the door. Maybe that would be funny; I'm not sure.

The notion of "penis envy" is hilarious. Please! Be serious! Why would we want a penis, when our business is all tucked away neatly inside, where it ought to be?

Roz Chast

"Howard is purely fictional. Any resemblance to a person living or dead is merely coincidental."

"You might have seen Judy's uterus on a recent PBS special."

Modern Love

WE DANCE AROUND EACH OTHER, trying to be noticed. While courtship rituals routinely shift over the centuries, each new wave of lovers tops the previous one in innovation. As we try to win each other over, the current generational displacement of love rituals now is almost a dislodgement. Flowers, candy, candlelit dinners, *romance*—while not totally a thing of the past—are being usurped by e-cards and texts. Eliciting attention from a love interest is realized with myriad technological advances. It wasn't too long ago that spouses were chosen for women by their parents. Now we are helping our parents choose a mate over the Internet.

Dating is now done through cyberspace, with a timer, or not at all. We blog to one another, link each other on our sites. And that fine line between dating and hanging out is blurred. Definitions are blurred. Hooking up, sexual intercourse don't mean one thing—it depends on what, who, where, and how. Answering instant messages—or not—speaks volumes, as does *how* you answer them. MySpace pictures tell stories. Things that were previously done in person are done in a million other ways. Our communication has increased, and the subtleties, while often leading to missed chances, are hard to keep up with. Picture cues, smiley faces—does he like me? Is he making fun of me? Do I even *like* someone who uses smiley faces in his e-mails? Can I *love* someone whose screen name is "boop123"?

But nothing beats chemistry. With all the advances, we still can't explain chemistry. Pheromones, hormones, cell phones—all won't give us the answer as to whom we will love. Scientific advances and computer vetting only reveal so much, and what is revealed may only confuse. You know it when you know it. And when you know it, IM him a YouTube link of yourself, smiling. And don't forget to link him on your site.

"If you think you've earned this by posting constructive comments on my blog—you're right."

"I'm planning on upgrading my lover and my computer.
But not necessarily in that order."

"Loves me . . . loves me not . . . loves me and another man."

"I'm totally into spontaneity, too, after the prerequisite blood tests."

"*Lately I'm not in a phallic mood, but in a vagina mood.*"

"What started as a hookup spun out of control into occasional dating."

"We had a gay marriage, a gay separation, and a gay divorce. Now we're managing a gay reconciliation."

ARE WOMEN FUNNY? SHOULD THEY BE?

It is a long-suppressed biblical fact that the first joke ever heard was made in the Garden of Eden by Eve. It was yet another beautiful day in Paradise when Eve plucked a glossy apple from the Tree of Knowledge. She took one bite, looked up, and spied Adam. She took a second more generous bite and realized for the first time that Adam wasn't wearing pants. Eve made a remark and laughed. Suddenly the sky darkened, there was crashing thunder and exploding lightning, clearly God was not pleased. He expelled Eve from the garden and condemned her thereafter to pain in childbirth. (He also granted her multiple orgasms, which proves that on one level he appreciates a good chuckle.) Adam followed Eve out of the Garden like a little puppy dog. Sadly, in all the commotion, he never got as much as a nibble of forbidden fruit. Which is why, even today, men tend to be on the clueless side and skittish around funny women.

Barbara Smaller

"*We met on the Internet, progressed to e-mail, then voice mail,
long-term I see us meeting in a public space for coffee.*"

"*I think we could be really bad for each other.*"

"I love you and I want to spend the rest of my marriage with you!"

"It turns out Ed and I like each other better online than offline."

"Learn to share!"

"Between two evils, I always pick the one I've never tried before."

Mae West

"Hold it. I need to take your photo so I can keep track of who I was with."

"Wake up, Dave, you can't spend the night on our first date."

"You met online? How quaint."

"I told you never to call me here."

"I think he really likes me. I told him I was just a regular girl who enjoys having sex, taping it, and sharing it with people on amateur porn sites."

"So now you're going to tell me what friends I can have?"

"Well, you'll just have to teach me about the Arctic monkeys, won't you?"

"But is really, really, really hating dating a strong enough basis for marriage?"

"Romantic love is a mental illness. But it's a pleasurable one, it's a drug. It distorts reality."

Fran Lebowitz

"Nothing could be better than being right here, now, with you, except, possibly, being right over there now with her."

"Put me on your do-not-call list."

"I've dated eleven enigmas—I want an open book."

"He left me for a pair of chopsticks—the bastard."

"He _said_ that he is socially liberal and fiscally conservative, but what he meant is that he sleeps around and is cheap."

MY MOTHER WAS A SHOE DESIGNER, and at the age of three I imitated her at her drawing board, creating cool women wearing fabulous shoes. So at first, I think I became a cartoonist because I loved to draw, and had fun creating my own little universe of groovy stylish women.

Now I realize that cartooning has become kind of my Prozac, Zoloft, or Ambien. Laughing about life is better than crying about it. It's less addictive than antidepressants, and less expensive than shopping therapy. (I should admit, however, that I have a shoe addiction.)

Finding the humor in everyday life has made me a happier person. I believe this, even though "some cartoonists have the dispositions of gravediggers," as the legendary cartoonist Frank Modell once said. My attitude toward humor came in handy when I was diagnosed with breast cancer, because, I think, in a weird way, I drew myself healthy. Who knows—I may have saved my own life.

The questions is, always: What separates people who survive and those who are unlucky enough not to make it? Yet because I drew myself as a VIXEN and not a *victim,* literally victoriously kicking cancer, I think I am alive today.

That's what I would say is the greatest thing about being a cartoonist. We have the ability to visualize our world, our life, and—in essence—be our own Creator.

And maybe we're all control freaks with God complexes.

Marisa Acocella Marchetto

"That's the best text I ever had."

"*I'd like to start spending more time with my cell phone.*"

*"You're more and more slovenly, out of shape, and insensitive!
If you're straight, just say so!"*

"Louise, do you promise not to wiretap, surreptitiously videotape, or photograph George?"

"Am I having an affair? Why? Am I allowed?"

"I told you Evan and I had an amicable divorce."

"*You do realize my husband will kill us if he catches us smoking in here.*"

"*Even more romantic than renewing our vows,
we're revising our prenup.*"

"Oh, okay. I'll let you win the battle if you let me win the war."

Cartoonists

ROZ CHAST

I WAS BORN IN BROOKLYN, New York, in 1954. My father was a high school teacher and my mother was an assistant principal. I was an only child and grew up in a small apartment in a nondescript and depressing part of Brooklyn.

I always loved to draw and really loved drawing in a cartoony way. With cartooning, you get to use pictures and words, which I liked. I never really thought much about what I wanted to do "for a living." I just knew I really, really loved to draw and make myself laugh and make others laugh, too.

My color sense was formed by Crayola crayons. My favorite colors were: blue-green, carnation pink, maroon, and black. I always wanted silver, copper, and gold to look as good on paper as they did in crayon form, but they never did. I hated the weird colors like blue-gray or salmon or bittersweet—I remember thinking that they looked grimy and sad, but now I like them better than the others. Those are probably adult colors. The combination of green and purple used to actually crack me up. It was so preposterous.

Growing up, I loved things that were funny. I loved *Mad* magazine. I was nuts about Don Martin, Dave Berg, and especially all the fake ads they ran. I liked Archie and his pals, even though I had to sneak reading about them at friends' houses because my parents were very anti-comic-book. I had no use for the Marvel superheroes; I thought they were boring. My parents subscribed to *The New Yorker.* When I was about eight or so, I discovered Charles Addams and fell in love with his cartoons. I really liked his books: *Black Maria, Monster Rally, Addams and Evil, Drawn and Quartered,* et cetera. When I was about thirteen, I saw Zap Comix for the first time, and that was another falling-in-love moment. I also loved Edward Gorey. I loved a lot of the cartoonists in the "Funny Pages" in the back of the old *National Lampoon,* especially Gahan Wilson. And I started to be old enough to actually read *The New Yorker,* where I realized I loved George Booth and Saul Steinberg and Sam Gross and William Steig and Ed Koren and many, many others. Later, I discovered Helen Hokinson and Mary Petty, which was great, because there weren't tons of women out there.

I went to Midwood High School, where I doodled my way through every class when I wasn't looking at the clock watching the second hand creep around in a very painful, almost psychedelically slow way. Then I went to Kirkland College, an experimental women's college, for two years. One would have been plenty, but I had a boyfriend. Et cetera. Then I went to RISD for four years, where I majored in Graphic Design, then Illustration, and finally Painting. I wanted to be an Artist with a capital *A,* but I wasn't serious enough, and also my paintings were god-awful.

When I got out of RISD, I moved back to New York and spent a lot of time working on a portfolio of illustration-y stuff, and also drawing cartoons, mostly for myself. I had a little bit of luck with the illustrations, but not much. I never thought the cartoons were commercially viable, but at a certain point I started showing them instead of the illustrations. *The Village Voice,* the *National Lampoon,* and a small magazine called *Christopher Street* were my first markets. When I was twenty-three, I dropped a portfolio of cartoons off at *The New Yorker* and much to my surprise, Lee Lorenz, the art editor at the time, told me that they were going to buy a cartoon, and that I should start coming back with my cartoons every Wednesday. Which I did.

I can't believe this many years has passed, but that's essentially what I'm still doing. Other than that, I have two children who are almost grown up, and I live in suburbia.

I guess that's it.

LIZA DONNELLY

WASHINGTON, DC—MY HOMETOWN— is a fertile breeding ground for a cartoonist, particularly if one grows up in the middle of the civil rights movement, the second wave of feminism, Vietnam, and Watergate. Luckily, I found drawing early in life, and spent my time creating humorous pictures to amuse myself and make my parents laugh. We lived abroad for a while, an experience that

DONNELLY

sealed my cartoon life—it gave me perspective that I might not have had otherwise. I spent much time alone, at sixteen, wandering, observing people: an outsider.

While at college, I wrote Andy Logan, city correspondent at *The New Yorker* and a family friend. I asked her if she would mind forwarding some of my work to the art editor. She wrote back and said sure and that she had been asking (art editor) Lee Lorenz why there weren't more women artists, and did he know why. Logan wrote to me that Lorenz was always looking for new talent, and that I might have a chance. Not surprisingly, I didn't sell at that point, but it was the first time I thought of myself as a *woman cartoonist,* not simply a cartoonist, a realization that lay dormant for years.

My influences have varied, but began with James Thurber, Dr. Seuss, Crockett Johnson, and Charles Schultz. I learned to draw cartoons because of James Thurber, tracing his work when I was little. When I was a young nonreader, Crockett Johnson's early graphic novel *Barnaby* allowed me to read a *book* with great pride. When I discovered Dr. Seuss, I thought I had died and gone to heaven. The wry but caring humor of Schultz spoke to me every day in the newspapers. Cartooning became *mine,* very early on. It was my identity. In my early years of drawing, there weren't women cartoonists to whom I looked for inspiration, partly because I didn't think of it that way. I just looked at drawings that I loved, and the gender of the artist was irrelevant—really as it should be. Not to mention there weren't many women publishing cartoons.

The New Yorker bought a cartoon from me not long after I moved to New York City after college. I had a wonderful job for a few years in the Art Department of the American Museum of Natural History (biology was my other passion) while I built my career in cartooning. Even though I wanted to be a political cartoonist, as I got over my college-bred Marxism I realized that *The New Yorker* was indeed political, and that some of its artists were voicing opinions.

Since then, my work has appeared in many national publications, anthologies, and exhibitions.

I edited four cartoon collections (three with Michael Maslin), and wrote and illustrated seven children's books for Scholastic about dinosaurs. Writing a history of women cartoonists, *Funny Ladies:* The New Yorker's *Greatest Women Cartoonists and Their Cartoons* (Prometheus Books) was an absolute labor of love that I didn't want to end. Luckily, I conceived of this present volume, which has been an equally wonderful experience. In 2006, I was invited to speak to and be a part of an international group of political cartoonists at the United Nations in an initiative called Cartooning for Peace. With the traveling exhibition, we continue to speak worldwide, and I am working on a book about the effort with Emory University. When not drawing and putting books together, I teach at Vassar College.

Michael Maslin, another *New Yorker* cartoonist, and I married in the middle of all of the above. We have two daughters whom we try very hard to raise with a lot of laughs.

CAROLITA JOHNSON

CAROLITA JOHNSON GREW UP in Queens, New York, where attempts were made to persuade her that this was all there was, and then you die. An attempt was made on her own initiative—in case this turned out to be true—to stall this inevitability by going to the Parsons School of Design and getting a BFA. Just when she was about to throw in the towel and get a job on Seventh Avenue and a mortgage and wait for marriage, kids, and death, she bet all for nothing and bought a one-way ticket to London.

Carolita hated London. So she moved to Paris, France, where she modeled for five years as part of the "ugly" or "real person" model movement, which didn't do much for her self-esteem but paid the rent on her various hot-water- and interior-toilet-deprived garrets. When that movement petered out, she persuaded the French government to give her free education in the national university system, which she took full advantage of for five years.

Five years later, with several (not very useful, but worthy) degrees and several diverse jobs under her belt, Carolita was invited by the French to return to her country of origin and get a life. Upon her return to New York, she got a job working for various renowned photographers. After two years of

CAROLITA ON A TYPICAL DAY

KNAPSACK, CONTAINING: MAGAZINE, PAPER, MOIST TOWELETTES, PURSE, MAKEUP

FEMININE HYGEINE PRODUCTS, ALLERGY PILLS, PENS, PENCILS, SUNSCREEN, WHITE-OUT, SKETCH-BOOK, TRAIN SCHEDULE, COMPASS, HANDBALL, MINI FLASH-LIGHT.

UTRECHT TOTE BAG WITH: BAG O'BOOBS (BRA INSERTS, EXTRA BRA, THONG, TANK TOP, LEGGINGS), MOBY DICK, HIGH HEELS.

CELL PHONE (CONTAINING VOICE MEMOS OF IDEAS, AND TEXT MESSAGES TO SELF, PHOTOS OF SLEEPING SUBWAY PASSENGERS, VARIOUS BARNYARD RINGERS.)

this, as well as some subversive and self-financed artistic activities, she was ten grand in debt and decided that if she was going to be kicked around for only thirty grand a year by bosses who spent vacations with celebrities in posh places while she toiled away her best years with an aging Spanish mutt named Carmen, she'd rather do it in France under the auspices of an "employee contract for life" and national health insurance. Which is what she did for another two years, as an international software tester.

The French were very good to her, but one day Carolita realized that it had been thirteen years since she'd decided that artistic talent was nothing without experience and left home in search of the latter. She returned to New York with the intention of becoming an illustrator—maybe even a cartoonist—and thanks to the encouragement of a fellow cartoonist sold her first cartoon within five weeks. The moral of that story is: Timing is everything (and, just as important: Don't believe everything your family or friends tell you until you check their credentials).

Carolita continues to contribute cartoons to *The New Yorker,* and does illustrations for other clients, as well as portraits and oil paintings. She continues to model, has a blog at www.newyorkette.com, and is working on a graphic novel, just like everyone else and their mother.

MARISA ACOCELLA MARCHETTO

TO BE HONEST, I really wanted to be a rock star. When I was a student at Pratt Art Institute, I was the bass player in a punk band called the French Blues. Yeah, I know it's a lousy name, and we weren't so good at our instruments, but we somehow managed to open up for the B-52s once. Woohooo. How did that happen? We had a great lead singer with an amazing presence. Hey, I couldn't do it, because I didn't have a voice.

I dropped out of art school and went into advertising, where I worked my way up the corporate food chain, starting as an intern-slash-amoeba. Later, I admit I became kind of a big fish as founder of Kirshenbaum Bond & Partners. There, everyone thought I was taking copious notes in meetings. Actually, I was drawing—sketching women. Advertising was frustrating, because no matter what idea I had—whether print or television—it was always secondary to selling the product. I felt like a salesman in creative clothes. I felt I didn't have a voice. I left Kirshenbaum and went on to be a senior vice president at Young & Rubicam, where I became even more frustrated. In one of those many meetings, I once again drew one of the "women," this time with a gun in her mouth . . . surprising even myself.

New Year's Eve, a few weeks later, when I had just turned thirty, I was lighting votive candles and calling out to all the Higher Spirits I could think of, pleading for them to guide me out of a career that I didn't really like. As I prayed to God, Jesus, Mary, Joseph, Allah, Buddha, St. Anthony, St. Clare, and St. Philomena, I started drawing, and again drew that woman with a gun in her mouth, I wrote a line above her that said, "She was a little upset during the meeting . . ." It was my eureka moment!!!!! I FOUND MY VOICE!!!!

In that split second, I leaned into my sketchpad and what happened?

My hair caught on FIRE. (A word of caution: Be careful with epiphanies and votive candles.)

I developed a cartoon character called SHE, which ran in *Mirabella* magazine for three years, the first ongoing comic strip in a woman's magazine. SHE became a graphic novel, *Just Who the Hell Is She Anyway?,* and was developed as a pilot by HBO, but unfortunately never went to series.

Then I started cartooning for magazines, like *The New Yorker, ESPN* (I did a cartoon called *ESPioNage*), *Ad Age* (I had a weekly cartoon called *MAD AVE*), and a ton of others before I wound up at *The New York Times* as a roving cartoonist-slash-journalist, drawing a strip called *The Strip* (the *Times*'s first ongoing cartoon). In 2002, I began doing *Glamour Girls* for *Glamour,* a single-panel cartoon I'm still doing today.

It was for *Glamour* that I created *Cancer Vixen.* In May 2004, I was diagnosed with breast cancer three weeks before getting married. *Cancer Vixen* then became a graphic memoir (Knopf) in September 2006. It won the Medical Book of the Year award from Slate, was on Time.com's Best Graphic Novels of the Year list, was nominated for the Books for a Better Life Award, nominated by the National Cartoonists Society for Graphic Novel of the Year, and is being translated into many different languages. (I did get married. I had bandages from the lumpectomy underneath my wedding dress.)

Proudly, I have found a way to give back. I created a fund for women who don't have health insurance (the Cancer Vixen Fund at St. Vincent's Comprehensive Cancer Center). On National Mammography Day we sponsor free mammograms. The fund has already saved lives.

And work? I'm back at the drawing board writing a graphic novel, listening to my voice.

VICTORIA ROBERTS

I WAS BORN IN NEW YORK CITY; we moved to Mexico City when I was four and to Sydney, Australia, when I was thirteen. I returned to New York City in 1988, and have lived here happily, ever since.

I mention these places, my three "homes"—one American, one Mexican, and one Australian—because I love them all, still, and because living in each has made me the cartoonist that I am. Being an insider in too many cultures, and an outsider in all of them, too, has forced me to be an observer. Wherever I am, I am from somewhere else. To complicate matters further, I went to a French school.

My first loves were Babar and Tintin, and a book called *Le Petit Nicolas* illustrated by J. J. Sempé. When the 1968 Olympics were held in Mexico City, I had a poster by *New Yorker* artist Abel Quezada for the occasion. And in the guest bathroom, off my stepfather's library in Mexico City, were enough *New Yorker*s to keep me out of sight, in cartoons, and away from family dramas for hours on end.

When we moved to Australia and I was horribly homesick, the light at the end of the tunnel was Bruce Petty. I discovered his work in English class when our teacher projected Bruce's animated film *Australian History* on the classroom wall. Born and bred in Australia, Bruce worked as a cartoonist for the British magazine *Punch* as well as *The New Yorker.*

When I was sixteen, I spent the summer working at Film Graphics, an animation studio in Sydney. Thanks to the studio's head, David Deneen, who showed me that my work might be animated, I began to do storyboards, to put words to my drawings. I loved *Sesame Street* as well as the sitcom *Taxi* and Woody Allen films, and dreamed of going back to New York City. I wrote stories in "Noo Yawk" accents, and so was born the old couple I draw in *The New Yorker* today.

Bored at school, I left in eleventh grade or "fifth form," went to work at Hanna-Barbera's Sydney studio as a cel painter—and then went briefly to the National Art School, majoring in printmaking. The Australian government was very generous to filmmakers at the time, and I received a grant to create *Goodbye Sally Goldstein,* a short animated film. Working as a geriatric nurse on weekends at Mosman Nursing Home in Sydney, I worked on the film, and little by little, a few of my cartoons began to be published in Australian papers.

Seeing my work in print was an education. I learned more about work by being in print than by any other means. I don't feel a piece (a cartoon or any other artwork for that matter) is complete until it is "seen." What people bring to the work is essential; what is originally something tiny and personal, if it hits a chord, transforms into something much more valuable.

At nineteen, I created a cartoon strip based on biographies of famous figures, *My Sunday.* It ran in Australia and eventually in Holland, among other places. And that led to a three-book contract with Chatto & Windus, a British publisher.

I left the nursing home—the work was heavy, and I was never that good at it. But the experience gave me Nona Appleby, my oldest character—that is, she has been with me the longest. Nona is an eighty-six-year-old Australian lady, and were it not for the experience of hearing the dialogue of the older Aussies every weekend, I doubt she would be with me today. Nona's voice and her wisdom have accompanied me throughout my working life, fortunately. She is a lot smarter than I am, so I let her do her own thing. At the moment she has me playing her live on stage, so I have gone through my cartoons into acting in theater and on film. I have had to learn to speak Spanish, dance, play the cello, and sing Sondheim, skills Nona requires in her act. Work takes me by the hand and leads me, rather than it being the other way around.

Working for a British publisher gave me the courage, and the income, to move from Sydney to New York. The original manuscript of my first book for Chatto burned in a lorry accident, and I got the insurance money, five thousand pounds—my start!

New York was terrifying, but thanks to (among other folk) Michelle Urry, who was the cartoon editor of *Playboy,* and Jerelle Kraus who published my work on the op-ed page of *The New York Times,* I got ahead. Michelle didn't buy my work (because "Hef" never went for it), but she gave me the affirmation I needed to continue working. Even after a successful career in Australia, I was not sure I had the goods for what I considered the capital of the work world, NYC. I submitted to *The New Yorker* for one year, and gave up after many rejection slips. Then I started submitting cartoons and cover ideas on a weekly basis again, and I have been under contract to the magazine for twenty years.

My working life is so rich that I wonder if it shields me from "real life" somewhat. I feel immensely privileged to be doing the work I love and, further, to know it is well received. And within the world of my cartoons, like a soap opera or telenovela I might be addicted to, I can't wait to know what happens next.

BARBARA SMALLER

BARBARA SMALLER WAS BORN AND RAISED in one of the lesser parts of the Greater Chicago area. She was the second of six children. Her father often said in his jovial way that raising children was like training puppies. Even now she flinches just a bit at the sight of a tightly rolled-up newspaper. Her father was a funny man but the real comedian in the family was her mother, who at random moments would channel Lucy Ricardo. This would scare the younger children sometimes to tears, but delight the older ones who were "on to" the joke. While not a particularly domestic woman,

she was a conscientious mother who made sure her brood always had a wholesome breakfast. Barbara remembers many a morning running out the door with her siblings to catch the school bus and ducking as her mother, standing in her slippers on the front steps, flung out fistfuls of Cheerios and Rice Krispies.

Barbara came of age in that tumultuous nanosecond after the breakup of the Beatles but before disco changed our world forever. Interestingly, while she did not have a favorite Beatle, she did have a favorite *Gilligan's Island* castaway (okay, it was the Professor). She was in nursing school for about a minute and a half and then went on to work at numerous jobs and attend many universities. One of her favorite jobs was at the Art Institute of Chicago, where she broke the gender barrier by becoming one of the first women hired as a night guard, opening the way for all little girls with big dreams of wearing a jumpsuit with many pockets and zippers and carrying a disturbingly phallic flashlight. Her scariest job was as a resident counselor at a halfway house, where a few "clients" wished her bodily harm, though she was assured it was nothing personal. Her next most scary job was as a stand-up comic where many also wished her bodily harm and it was personal.

Along the way a gypsy said, "Why not try cartooning?" Soon her cartoons began appearing in *National Lampoon, Cosmopolitan,* and the *Guardian,* where she had a weekly cartoon panel titled *White Collar Crimes.* In 1996, she finally succumbed to the pleadings of *The New Yorker* magazine to be allowed to publish her drawings. Since then her cartoons have appeared regularly in that magazine and have been included in many anthologies. She is also a cartoonist for HealthCare-NOW, an advocacy group for national health insurance. She currently lives in New York City with her husband, daughter, and their dog, who has recently been diagnosed with OCD but is doing well with a combination of medication and talk therapy.

JULIA SUITS

I WAS BORN IN ST. LOUIS, the eldest of five children, to artist parents a few years before Sputnik orbited earth. As a girl, I was an earnest but cautious tomboy who climbed the lower branches of trees and studied snakes instead of killing them. My parents, former students of Max Beckmann and Philip Guston, painted daily. Their art filled the house, as did books and magazines—*The New Yorker* among them. My siblings and I made art when we weren't watching *Sea Hunt,* outside catching beetles, or playing a Midwestern version of stickball. A most cherished childhood possession was my baseball glove, autographed by Stan Musial when I was eleven. On that day in 1962, Musial looked me straight in the eye and told me that if I practiced hard enough I could make the major leagues. I believed him—until I was twelve, when I got hit square in the throat by a lame, high-bouncing grounder during a game of girls' softball. The next five years were spent denying puberty, obsessing over the Beatles, and trying to figure out what it really meant to be female. (Can it really be *this* bad?)

In the summer of Woodstock, and with money earned from summers of waitressing, I bought a '51 Chevy and moved to Madison, Wisconsin, for college, where I became a fringe participant in a culture of drugs, music, antiwar protests, free love, and whatever my studies were. Graduate school and medical illustration training followed, yet woven into that decade of schooling was a real-life education: hitchhiking across the country, living in strange places, and having some very unusual jobs. In the mid-1980s, I accepted a position as a medical illustrator and moved to Minneapolis, finally putting the seal on years of semi-purposeful aimlessness. I got married and had children, adjusting happily to motherhood but not to the cold. Even so, life indoors proved well suited to focused drawing, and I soon began a long association with Creators Syndicate in 1988. Eighteen years of making portraits for newspapers greatly improved my drawing skills. One day—two years ago—after a protracted bout of restlessness, I decided to try something new, and in 2006 my first cartoon was published in *The New Yorker.*

ANN TELNAES

ANN TELNAES is a Pulitzer Prize–winning editorial cartoonist whose work is nationally and internationally syndicated. Of Norwegian descent, Ann became a US citizen in her teenage years,

avoiding the future controversy over illegal Norwegian immigrants swarming the US borders and taking all the jobs Americans aren't willing to do. Trained as a character animator at California Institute of the Arts, Ann worked at various studios in Los Angeles, New York, London, and Taipei before making another financially brilliant career move into the notoriously low-paying profession of freelance editorial cartooning.

In 2004, the Library of Congress held an exclusive exhibition of Ann's editorial cartoons in conjunction with the publication of Humor's Edge: Cartoons by Ann Telnaes (Library of Congress and Pomegranate Press). A second cartoon collection of Vice President Dick Cheney—the man she can't get out of her mind—was published in 2007. Since completing *Dick*, Ann has been living in an undisclosed location in or near Washington, DC, with her husband, dogs, and a slightly overweight cat.

KIM WARP

KIM WARP IS A MARRIED MOTHER of two teenage girls. Her work has appeared in a wide variety of publications ranging from *The New Yorker, Barron's,* and *Harvard Business Review* to *Cosmopolitan, Reader's Digest,* and *National Lampoon.* In 2000, she was the recipient of the National Cartoonists Society's Gag Cartoon Division award. Her work has been included in many cartoon collections, including *Funny Ladies* and *The Rejection Collection.*

Kim has loved magazine cartoons since she was a small child in the 1960s. When normal children were outside playing, she would spend hours looking at her parents' *Collier's Collects Its Wits,* which was loaded with early cartoons by such greats as Charles Addams, Whitney Darrow Jr., and Richard Taylor. Kim was especially thrilled with the self-caricatures and biographies of the cartoonists (which is ironic, as creating self-caricatures and biographies is now among the things she dreads most). The best part was discovering that there were women cartoonists.

She currently resides in Virginia Beach with her family and an ever-changing array of pets.

SIGNE WILKINSON

HAVING BEEN BORN in the depths of the baby boom and then acquiring a BA in English from a western university of middling academic reputation, I was unprepared for real work . . . so I became a reporter. I also worked for the Quakers, for the Academy of Natural Sciences of Philadelphia, and with a peace-building project in Cyprus that ended nine months later, when war broke out.

Back home, I realized cartooning combined my interests in art and politics without taxing my interest in spelling. After much remedial art school, I began freelancing, finally landing a full-time job at the *San Jose Mercury News.* After a few years on a steep learning curve, I repaid my long-suffering editor by taking a job at the *Philadelphia Daily News,* where I have been drawing contentedly ever since.

My intensely unremarkable family life includes growing outdoor lilies, killing indoor orchids, finding an easy way to match my husband's socks, and trying to figure out the best way to answer the question, "What do you do all day after you finish drawing your cartoon?"

Credits

The drawings by Ann Talnaes, "Critics claim HPV vaccination will lead to promiscuity" (page 184) and "Having a baby at age 60—how ridiculous. Can't she just accept getting older?" (page 191) are reprinted courtesy of Women's enews, www.womensenewsorg.

Of the two hundred drawings in this book, twenty-eight originally appeared in *The New Yorker* and were copyrighted 1994–2007, inclusive, by The New Yorker Magazine. Grateful acknowledgment is made to *The New Yorker* for permission to reprint.

Acknowledgments

This book would not have been possible without the expert guidance and inspiration of my agent, David Kuhn, and my editor, Jonathan Karp. I would also like to thank Billy Kingsley, Nate Gray, Cary Goldstein, Carolyn Mimran, Tareth Mitch, Merredith Miller, Rita Henley-Jensen, and my editor at *The New Yorker,* Bob Mankoff. The cartoonists in this book have been amazing in the speed with which they responded to my requests, and their willingness to jump into this venture with me. I am very grateful for their thoughtfulness, creativity, and flexibility. And of course, I am forever grateful to my daughters, Ella and Gretchen, for their love and patience as I worked late into the night, and to my father for a lifetime of encouragement and support. Last but not least, thanks go to my partner in life and cartooning, Michael, for being my house-husband and confidant, cheering me on every time I try something new.

ABOUT TWELVE

TWELVE

TWELVE was established in August 2005 with the objective of publishing no more than one book per month. We strive to publish the singular book, by authors who have a unique perspective and compelling authority. Works that explain our culture; that illuminate, inspire, provoke, and entertain. We seek to establish communities of conversation surrounding our books. Talented authors deserve attention not only from publishers, but from readers as well. To sell the book is only the beginning of our mission. To build avid audiences of readers who are enriched by these works—that is our ultimate purpose.

For more information about forthcoming TWELVE books, you can visit us at www.twelvebooks.com.